CONTENTS

KV-194-975

Introduction

From the hot, spicy dishes of Szechuan to the aromatic Crispy Duck of Beijing, the cooking of China offers a fascinating range of delicious dishes for you to create in your own kitchen. Once you have mastered one or two basic principles, you'll appreciate the speed and ease with which Chinese food can be cooked.

There are four regional schools of Chinese cooking and each gives cooks the world over a set of distinctive flavours and aromas. Cantonese is the best known of these cuisines, and uses light and subtle flavourings in contrast to the fiery Szechaun dishes and the rich Shanghai recipes. Beijing cuisine depends more on dried and smoked ingredients due to the harsh winters in that area.

When planning a meal allow one dish per person to give variety and colour to your table. Remember to cook some dishes in advance and others just before the meal, otherwise you might find you don't sit down while your guests eat.

The recipes appear in the order in which they are usually eaten: first come appetizers like Money Bags and Spring Rolls, then soups, which combine all sorts of delicious flavours. Fish and seafood follow, and then the poultry and meats. Lastly come accompaniments to the main dishes, including Egg Fried Rice and Ma-Po Tofu. Many of these dishes will complement each other, so don't feel obliged to stick to courses – there is nothing more satisfying than seeing ten fragrant and delicious dishes on a table, waiting to be eaten.

Spring Rolls

Spring roll wrappers are available from oriental shops and some supermarkets.

MAKES 12

5 Chinese dried mushrooms (or open-cup mushrooms)
1 large carrot • 60 g/2 oz/1 cup canned bamboo shoots
2 spring onions (scallions) • 60 g/2 oz Chinese leaves
2 tbsp vegetable oil • 250 g/8 oz/4 cups bean-sprouts
1 tbsp soy sauce • 12 spring roll wrappers
1 egg, beaten • vegetable oil for deep-frying • salt

1 Place the mushrooms in a small bowl and cover with warm water. Leave to soak for 20–25 minutes. Drain the mushrooms and squeeze out the excess water. Remove the tough centres and slice the mushrooms fairly thinly. Cut the carrot and bamboo shoots into very thin julienne strips. Chop the spring onions (scallions) and shred the Chinese leaves.

2 Heat the 2 tablespoons of oil in a wok or frying pan (skillet). Add the mushrooms, carrot and bamboo shoots, and stir-fry for 2 minutes. Add the spring onions (scallions), Chinese leaves, bean-sprouts and soy sauce. Season with salt and stir-fry for 2 minutes. Leave to cool.

Divide the mixture into 12 equal portions and place one portion on the edge of each spring roll wrapper. Fold in the sides and roll each one up, brushing the join with a little beaten egg to seal.

3 Heat the oil in a wok or large saucepan to 180–190°C/350–375°F or until a cube of bread browns in 30 seconds. Deep-fry the spring rolls in batches for 4–5 minutes, until golden and crispy. If the oil is too hot the rolls will brown on the outside before cooking on the inside. Remove and drain on paper towels. Keep each batch of rolls warm while the others are being cooked. Serve at once.

Money Bags

Try dipping these steamed dumplings in a mixture of soy sauce, sherry and slivers of ginger root.

SERVES 4

3 Chinese dried mushrooms (or thinly sliced open-cup mushrooms)
250 g/8 oz/2 cups plain (all-purpose) flour
1 egg, beaten • 75 ml/3 fl oz/⅓ cup water
1 tsp baking powder • ¾ tsp salt
2 tbsp vegetable oil • 2 spring onions (scallions), chopped
90 g/3 oz/½ cup sweetcorn kernels
½ red chilli, deseeded and chopped
1 tbsp brown bean sauce

1 Place the dried mushrooms in a small bowl, cover with warm water and leave to soak for 20–25 minutes. Remove the tough centres and chop the mushrooms.

2 To make the wrappers, sift the flour into a bowl. Add the egg and mix lightly. Stir in the water, baking powder and salt. Mix to a soft dough. Knead lightly until smooth on a floured board. Cover with a damp cloth and set aside for 5–6 minutes. This allows the baking powder time to activate, so that the dumplings swell when they are steamed.

3 Drain the mushrooms, squeezing them dry.

4 Heat the oil in a wok or large frying pan (skillet) and stir-fry the mushrooms, spring onions (scallions), sweetcorn and chilli for 2 minutes. Stir in the brown bean sauce and remove from the heat.

5 Roll the dough into a large sausage and cut into 24 even-sized pieces. Roll each piece out into a thin round and place a teaspoonful of the filling in the centre. Gather up the edges, pinch together and twist to seal.

6 Stand the dumplings in an oiled bamboo steamer. Place over a saucepan of simmering water, cover and steam for 12–14 minutes before serving.

Bang-Bang Chicken

The cooked chicken meat is tenderized by beating with a rolling pin, hence the name for this very popular Szechuan dish.

SERVES 4

1 litre/ 1¾ pints/ 4 cups water
2 chicken quarters (breast half and leg)
1 cucumber, cut into matchsticks

Sauce:
2 tbsp light soy sauce
1 tsp sugar
1 tbsp finely chopped spring onions (scallions)
1 tsp red chilli oil
¼ tsp pepper
1 tsp white sesame seeds
2 tbsp peanut butter, creamed with a little sesame oil

1 Bring the water to a rolling boil in a wok or a large pan. Add the chicken pieces, reduce the heat, cover and cook for 30–35 minutes.

2 Remove the chicken from the pan and immerse in a bowl of cold water for at least 1 hour to cool, ready for shredding.

3 Remove the chicken pieces and drain well. Pat dry with paper towels, then take the meat off the bone.

4 On a flat surface, pound the chicken with a rolling pin, then tear the meat into even-sized shreds with 2 forks. Mix the chicken with the shredded cucumber and arrange in a shallow serving dish.

5 To serve, mix together all the sauce ingredients and pour over the chicken.

Deep-Fried Spare Ribs

The spare ribs should be chopped into small bite-sized pieces before or after cooking.

SERVES 4

8–10 finger spare ribs
1 tsp five-spice powder or 1 tbsp mild curry powder
1 tbsp rice wine or dry sherry
1 egg • 2 tbsp flour
vegetable oil, for deep-frying
1 tsp finely shredded spring onions (scallions)
1 tsp finely shredded fresh green or red hot chillies, deseeded
salt and pepper

Spicy salt & pepper:
1 tbsp salt • 1 tsp five-spice powder
1 tsp ground Szechuan peppercorns

1 Chop the ribs into 3–4 small pieces. Place the ribs in a bowl with salt and pepper to taste, five-spice or curry powder and the wine or sherry. Turn to coat the ribs in the spices and leave them to marinate for 1–2 hours.

2 Make the Spicy Salt & Pepper by combining the ground spices in a small bowl.

3 Mix the egg and flour together to make a batter. Dip the ribs in the batter one by one. Heat the oil in a preheated wok until smoking. Deep-fry the ribs for 4–5 minutes, then remove with a slotted spoon, and drain on paper towels. Return the ribs to the hot oil and fry again for 1 minute. Remove and drain on paper towels again.

4 Pour 1 tablespoon of the hot oil over the spring onions (scallions) and chillies and leave for 30–40 seconds. Serve the ribs with Spicy Salt & Pepper, garnished with the shredded spring onions (scallions) and chillies.

Butterfly Prawns (Shrimp)

Use unpeeled, raw king or tiger prawns (jumbo shrimp) which are about 7–10 cm (3–4 inches) long.

SERVES 4

12 raw tiger prawns (jumbo shrimp) in their shells
2 tbsp light soy sauce
1 tbsp Chinese rice wine or dry sherry
1 tbsp cornflour (cornstarch)
vegetable oil for deep-frying
2 eggs, lightly beaten
8–10 tbsp breadcrumbs
salt and pepper
shredded lettuce leaves, to serve
chopped spring onions (scallions), to garnish

1 Shell and devein the prawns (shrimp) but leave the tails on. Split them in half from the underbelly about halfway along, leaving the tails still firmly attached.

2 Mix together the soy sauce, wine, cornflour (cornstarch), and salt and pepper in a bowl, add the prawns (shrimp) and turn to coat. Leave to marinate for 10–15 minutes.

3 Heat the oil in a preheated wok to 180–190°C/350–375°F or until a cube of bread browns in 30 seconds. Pick up each prawn (shrimp) by the tail, dip it in the beaten egg then roll it in the breadcrumbs to coat well.

4 Deep-fry the prawns (shrimp) in batches until golden brown. Remove with a slotted spoon and drain on paper towels.

5 To serve, arrange the prawns (shrimp) on a bed of lettuce leaves and garnish with spring onions (scallions), either raw or soaked in a tablespoon of the hot oil for about 30 seconds.

Wonton Soup

Filled wontons are served in a clear soup.

SERVES 4

Wonton skins:
1 egg • 6 tbsp water
250 g/ 8 oz/ 2 cups plain (all-purpose) flour

Filling:
125 g/ 4 oz/ ½ cup frozen chopped spinach, defrosted
15 g/½ oz/ 1 tbsp pine kernels (nuts), toasted and chopped
30 g/ 1 oz/ ¼ cup minced quorn (TVP) • salt

Soup:
600 ml/ 1 pint/ 2½ cups vegetable stock
1 tbsp dry sherry • 1 tbsp light soy sauce
2 spring onions (scallions), chopped

1 Beat the egg lightly in a bowl and mix with the water. Stir in the flour to form a stiff dough. Knead lightly, then cover with a damp cloth and leave to rest for 30 minutes. Roll the dough out into a large sheet about 5 mm/¼ inch thick. Cut out 24 × 7.5 cm/3 inch squares. Dust each one lightly with flour. Only 12 squares are required for the soup so freeze the remainder.

2 To make the filling, squeeze out the excess water from the spinach. Mix the spinach with the pine kernels (nuts) and quorn (TVP). Season with salt. Divide the mixture into 12 equal portions and place one portion in the centre of each square. Bring the opposite corners of the square together and squeeze to seal.

3 To make the soup, bring the stock, sherry and soy sauce to the boil, add the wontons and boil rapidly for 2–3 minutes. Add the spring onions (scallions) and serve in warmed soup bowls.

Hot & Sour Soup

This is the most popular soup in Chinese restaurants and homes throughout the world.

SERVES 4

4–6 dried Chinese mushrooms, soaked in warm water
for 30 minutes
125 g/ 4 oz cooked pork or chicken
1 cake tofu (bean curd)
60 g/ 2 oz canned sliced bamboo shoots, drained
600 ml/ 1 pint/ 2½ cups Chinese Stock (see page 20) or water
1 tbsp Chinese rice wine or dry sherry
1 tbsp light soy sauce
2 tbsp rice vinegar
salt and pepper
2–3 spring onions (scallions), sliced thinly, to serve

Cornflour (cornstarch) paste:
1 tbsp cornflour (cornstarch) • 1½ tbsp cold water

1 Drain the mushrooms, squeeze dry and discard the hard stalks. Thinly slice the mushrooms.

2 Thinly slice the meat, tofu (bean curd) and bamboo shoots into narrow shreds.

3 Make the cornflour (cornstarch) paste: blend the cornflour (cornstarch) with the water in a bowl until smooth.

4 Bring the stock or water to a rolling boil in a wok or large pan and add the mushrooms, meat, tofu (bean curd) and bamboo shoots. Return to the boil and simmer for about 1 minute. Add the wine, soy sauce, vinegar, salt and pepper. Bring back to the boil once more, stirring in the cornflour (cornstarch) paste to thicken the soup. Serve hot, sprinkled with the spring onions (scallions).

Three-Flavour Soup

If raw prawns (shrimp) are not available, add ready-cooked ones at the last stage. Left-over Chinese Stock can be kept in the refrigerator for 4–5 days or frozen.

SERVES 4

125 g/ 4 oz boned and skinned chicken breast
125 g/ 4 oz raw peeled prawns (shrimp)
½ egg white, beaten lightly
2 tsp Cornflour (Cornstarch) Paste (see page 18)
125 g/ 4 oz honey-roast ham • salt and pepper
finely chopped spring onions (scallions), to garnish

Chinese stock (makes 2.5 litres/4 pints/10 cups):
750 g/ 1½ lb chicken pieces • 750 g/ 1½ lb pork spare ribs
3.75 litres/ 6 pints/ 15 cups cold water
3–4 pieces of ginger root, crushed
3–4 spring onions (scallions), each tied into a knot
3–4 tbsp Chinese rice wine or dry sherry

1 Slice the chicken into thin shreds. If the prawns (shrimp) are large, cut each in half lengthways, otherwise leave whole. Place the chicken and prawns (shrimps) in a bowl and mix with a pinch of salt, the egg white and cornflour (cornstarch) paste until well coated.

2 Cut the ham into thin slices roughly the same size as the chicken pieces.

3 To make the Chinese Stock, trim off the excess fat from the chicken and spare ribs and chop into large pieces. Place the meat in a large pan with the water and add the ginger and spring onion (scallion) knots. Bring to the boil, and skim off the scum. Reduce the heat and simmer uncovered for 2–3 hours. Strain the stock through a collander, discarding the chicken, pork, ginger and spring onions

(scallions). Return the stock to the pan. Add the wine and simmer for 2–3 minutes.

raw prawns (shrimps) and the ham. Bring back to the boil, and simmer for 1 minute.

4 Put 750 ml/1¼ pints/ 3 cups stock or water in a pan and bring to a rolling boil. Add the chicken, the

5 Season with salt and pepper and serve the soup hot, garnished with the spring onions (scallions).

Pork & Szechuan Vegetable Soup

Sold in cans, Szechuan preserved vegetable is pickled mustard root which is quite hot and salty, so rinse in water before use.

SERVES 4

250 g/8 oz pork fillet
2 tsp Cornflour (Cornstarch) Paste (see page 18)
125 g/4 oz Szechuan preserved vegetable
750 ml/1¼ pints/3 cups Chinese Stock (see page 20)
or water
salt and pepper
a few drops of sesame oil (optional)
2–3 spring onions (scallions), sliced, to garnish

1 Cut the pork across the grain into thin shreds and mix with the cornflour (cornstarch) paste.

2 Wash and rinse the Szechuan preserved vegetable, then cut into thin shreds about the same size as the pork.

3 Bring the stock or water to a rolling boil in a wok or pan. Add the pork, stir to separate the shreds and bring back to the boil.

4 Add the Szechuan preserved vegetable and bring back to the boil once more. Season with salt and pepper and sprinkle with sesame oil (if using). Serve hot, garnished with spring onions (scallions).

Szechuan Prawns (Shrimp)

Use raw prawns (shrimp) if possible, otherwise omit steps 1 and 2 and add the cooked prawns (shrimp) before the sauce at step 3.

SERVES 4

250–300 g/ 8–10 oz raw tiger prawns (jumbo shrimp)
pinch of salt • ½ egg white, lightly beaten
1 tsp Cornflour (Cornstarch) Paste (see page 18)
600 ml/ 1 pint/ 2½ cups vegetable oil
fresh coriander (cilantro) leaves, to garnish

Sauce:
1 tsp finely chopped ginger root
2 spring onions (scallions), chopped finely
1 garlic clove, chopped finely
3–4 small dried red chillies, deseeded and chopped
1 tbsp light soy sauce • 1 tsp rice wine or dry sherry
1 tbsp tomato purée (paste) • 1 tbsp oyster sauce
2–3 tbsp Chinese Stock (see page 20) or water
a few drops of sesame oil

1 Peel the raw prawns (shrimp), then mix with the salt, egg white and cornflour (cornstarch) paste until coated all over.

2 Heat the oil in a preheated wok until it is smoking, then deep-fry the prawns (shrimp) for 1 minute. Remove with a slotted spoon and drain.

3 Pour off the oil, leaving about 1 tablespoon in the wok. Add all the ingredients for the sauce, bring to the boil and stir until smooth and well blended. Add the prawns (shrimp) to the sauce, stirring to blend. Garnish with coriander (cilantro) leaves.

Braised Fish Fillets

Any white fish such as lemon sole or plaice is ideal for this dish.

SERVES 4

3–4 small Chinese dried mushrooms
300–350 g/ 10–12 oz fish fillets • 1 tsp salt
½ egg white, lightly beaten
1 tsp Cornflour (Cornstarch) Paste (see page 18)
600 ml/ 1 pint/ 2½ cups vegetable oil
1 tsp finely chopped ginger root
2 spring onions (scallions), finely chopped
1 garlic clove, finely chopped
½ small green (bell) pepper, deseeded and cut into small cubes
½ small carrot, thinly sliced
60 g/ 2 oz canned sliced bamboo shoots, rinsed and drained
½ tsp sugar • 1 tbsp light soy sauce
1 tsp rice wine or dry sherry • 1 tbsp chilli bean sauce
2–3 tbsp Chinese Stock (see page 20) or water
a few drops of sesame oil

1 Soak the dried mushrooms in warm water for 30 minutes, then drain on paper towels, reserving the soaking water for stock or soup. Squeeze the mushrooms to extract all the moisture, cut off and discard any hard stems and slice thinly.

2 Cut the fish into bite-sized pieces, then place in a dish and mix with a pinch of salt, the egg white and cornflour (cornstarch) paste, turning the fish to coat. Heat the oil to 180–190°C/ 350–375°F or until a cube of bread browns in 30 seconds and deep-fry the fish for 1 minute. Remove with a slotted spoon and drain.

3 Pour off the oil, leaving 1 tablespoon in the wok. Add the ginger, spring onions (scallions) and garlic to flavour the oil for a few seconds, then add the vegetables and stir-fry for 1 minute.

4 Add the sugar, soy sauce, wine, chilli bean sauce, stock or water, and remaining salt, and bring to the boil. Add the fish pieces, stir to coat well with the sauce, and braise for 1 minute. Sprinkle with sesame oil and serve immediately.

Fried Squid Flowers

**The addition of green (bell) pepper
and black bean sauce to the squid makes
a colourful and delicious dish from the
Cantonese school.**

SERVES 4

*350–400 g/12–13 oz prepared and cleaned squid
1 green (bell) pepper, cored and deseeded
3–4 tbsp vegetable oil
1 garlic clove, chopped finely
¼ tsp finely chopped ginger root
2 tsp finely chopped spring onions (scallions)
½ tsp salt
2 tbsp crushed black bean sauce
1 tsp Chinese rice wine or dry sherry
a few drops of sesame oil*

1 Clean the squid by first cutting off the head. Cut off the tentacles and reserve. Remove the small soft bone at the base of the tentacles and the transparent backbone, as well as the ink bag. Peel off the thin skin, then wash and dry thoroughly. Open up the squid and score the inside of the flesh in a criss-cross pattern.

2 Cut the squid into pieces about the size of an oblong postage stamp. Blanch in a bowl of boiling water for a few seconds until all the pieces curl up. Drain and dry thoroughly on paper towels.

3 Cut the (bell) pepper into small triangular pieces. Heat the oil in a preheated wok and stir-fry the (bell) pepper for about 1 minute. Add the garlic, ginger, spring onions (scallions), salt and squid and stir-fry for 1 minute.

4 Finally, add the black bean sauce and wine, and blend well. Serve hot, sprinkled with sesame oil.

Baked Crab with Ginger

The crab is interchangeable with lobster. In Chinese restaurants, only live crabs and lobsters are used, but ready-cooked ones can be used at home.

SERVES 4

*1 large or 2 medium crabs,
weighing about 750 g/ 1½ lb in total
2 tbsp Chinese rice wine or dry sherry
1 egg, lightly beaten
1 tbsp cornflour (cornstarch)
3–4 tbsp vegetable oil
1 tbsp finely chopped ginger root
3–4 spring onions (scallions), cut into sections
2 tbsp light soy sauce
1 tsp sugar
75 ml/ 3 fl oz/ ⅓ cup Chinese Stock (see page 20) or water
½ tsp sesame oil
fresh coriander (cilantro) leaves, to garnish*

1 Cut the crab in half from the under-belly. Break off the claws and crack them with the back of a cleaver or large kitchen knife. Discard the legs and crack the shell, breaking it into several pieces. Discard the feathery gills and the stomach sac.

2 Place the crab pieces in a bowl with the wine, egg and cornflour (cornstarch) and leave to marinate for 10–15 minutes.

3 Heat the oil in a preheated wok and stir-fry the crab with the ginger and spring onions (scallions) for 2–3 minutes.

4 Add the soy sauce, sugar and stock or water, blend well and bring to the boil. Cover and cook for 3–4 minutes, then remove the lid. Sprinkle with sesame oil and garnish with fresh coriander (cilantro) leaves before serving.

Seafood Chow Mein

Use any seafood available for this delicious dish – mussels or crab would be suitable.

SERVES 4

90 g / 3 oz squid, cleaned • 3–4 fresh scallops
90 g / 3 oz raw prawns (shrimp), shelled
½ egg white, beaten lightly
1 tbsp Cornflour (Cornstarch) Paste (see page 18)
275 g / 9 oz egg noodles • 5–6 tbsp vegetable oil
2 tbsp light soy sauce • 60 g / 2 oz mangetout (snow peas)
½ tsp salt • ½ tsp sugar
1 tsp Chinese rice wine or dry sherry
2 spring onions (scallions), shredded finely
a few drops of sesame oil

1 Open up the squid and score the inside in a criss-cross pattern. Cut into pieces about the size of a postage stamp. Soak the squid in a bowl of boiling water until all the pieces curl up. Rinse in cold water and drain.

2 Cut each scallop into 3–4 slices. Cut the prawns (shrimp) in half lengthways if large. Mix the scallops and prawns with the egg white and cornflour (cornstarch) paste.

3 Cook the noodles in boiling water according to the instructions on the packet, then drain and rinse under cold water. Drain well, then toss with 1 tablespoon of oil.

4 Heat 3 tablespoons of oil in a preheated wok. Add the noodles and 1 tablespoon of the soy sauce and stir-fry for 2–3 minutes. Remove to a serving dish and keep warm.

5 Heat the remaining oil in the wok and add the mangetout (snow peas) and seafood. Stir-fry for about 2 minutes, then add the salt, sugar, wine, remaining soy sauce and about half the spring onions (scallions). Blend well and add a little stock or water if necessary.

6 Pour the seafood mixture on top of the noodles and sprinkle with sesame oil.

Garnish with the remaining spring onions (scallions) and serve hot or cold.

Aromatic & Crispy Duck

The pancakes traditionally served with this dish take ages to make. Buy ready-made ones, or use crisp lettuce instead.

SERVES 4

2 large duck quarters • 1 tsp salt
3–4 pieces star anise • 1 tsp Szechuan red peppercorns
1 tsp cloves • 2 cinnamon sticks, broken into pieces
2–3 spring onions (scallions), cut into short sections
4–5 small slices ginger root
3–4 tbsp rice wine or dry sherry
vegetable oil for deep-frying

To serve:

12 ready-made pancakes or 12 crisp lettuce leaves
hoi-sin or plum sauce • ¼ cucumber, shredded thinly
3–4 spring onions (scallions), shredded thinly

1 Rub the duck pieces with the salt and arrange the star anise, peppercorns, cloves and cinnamon on top. Sprinkle with the spring onions (scallions), ginger and wine and leave to marinate for at least 3–4 hours.

2 Arrange the duck pieces (with the marinade spices) on a plate that will fit inside a bamboo steamer. Pour some hot water into a wok, place the bamboo steamer in the wok, sitting on a trivet. Put in the duck and cover with the bamboo lid. Steam the duck pieces over a high heat for at least 2–3 hours, until tender and cooked through. Top up the hot water from time to time.

3 Remove the duck and leave to cool for at least 4–5 hours – this is very important, for unless the duck is cold and dry, it will not be very crispy.

4 Pour off the water and wipe the wok dry. Pour in the oil and heat until

smoking. Deep-fry the duck pieces, skin-side down, for 4–5 minutes or until crisp and brown. Remove and drain on paper towels.

5 To serve, scrape the meat off the bone, place about 1 teaspoon of hoi-sin or plum sauce on the centre of a pancake or lettuce leaf and add a few pieces of cucumber, spring onion (scallion) and duck meat. Wrap up to form a small parcel and eat with your fingers. Provide plenty of paper napkins for your guests.

Kung Po Chicken with Cashew Nuts

Peanuts, walnuts or almonds can be used instead of the cashew nuts, if preferred.

SERVES 4

250–300 g/ 8–10 oz boned and skinned chicken meat
¼ tsp salt
⅓ egg white
1 tsp Cornflour (Cornstarch) Paste (see page 18)
1 green (bell) pepper, cored and deseeded
4 tbsp vegetable oil
1 spring onion (scallion), cut into short sections
a few small slices of ginger root
4–5 small dried red chillies, soaked, deseeded and shredded
2 tbsp crushed yellow bean sauce
1 tsp rice wine or dry sherry
125 g/ 4 oz roasted cashew nuts
a few drops of sesame oil • boiled rice, to serve

1 Cut the chicken into small cubes about the size of sugar lumps. Place in a small bowl and mix with a pinch of salt, the egg white and the cornflour (cornstarch) paste, in that order. Cut the green (bell) pepper into cubes or triangles about the same size as the chicken pieces.

2 Heat the oil in a preheated wok, add the chicken cubes and stir-fry for about 1 minute, or until the colour changes. Remove the chicken with a slotted spoon and keep warm.

3 Add the spring onion (scallion), ginger, chillies and green (bell) pepper to the wok. Stir-fry for about 1 minute, then add the chicken with the yellow bean sauce and wine. Blend well and stir-fry for 1 minute. Finally stir in the cashew nuts and sesame oil. Serve hot, with boiled rice.

Lemon Chicken

Lemon sauce is a Cantonese speciality, easily available from oriental stores, or you can make your own.

SERVES 4

350 g/ 12 oz boned and skinned chicken breasts
1 tbsp rice wine or dry sherry
1 egg, beaten
4 tbsp plain (all-purpose) flour blended with 2 tbsp water
vegetable oil for deep-frying
salt and pepper
slices of fresh lemon, to garnish • boiled rice, to serve

Lemon sauce:
1 tbsp vegetable oil
250 ml/ 8 fl oz/ 1 cup Chinese Stock (see page 20) or water
1 tbsp caster sugar • 1 tbsp lemon juice
1 tbsp cornflour (cornstarch)
1 tsp salt • 1 tsp lemon rind

1 To make the lemon sauce, heat the oil in a wok until hot, reduce the heat and add all the other ingredients. Blend well, then boil and stir until smooth.

2 Cut the chicken into thin slices and place in a dish with wine, and salt and pepper. Leave to marinate for 25–30 minutes. Make a batter with the egg and the flour paste. Place the chicken slices in the batter and coat well.

3 Heat the oil in a wok or deep-fryer to 180–190°C/ 350–375°F or until a cube for bread browns in 30 seconds. Deep-fry the chicken until golden, remove and drain on paper towels. Cut the chicken slices into bite-sized pieces.

4 Heat 1 tablespoon of oil in a wok or pan. Stir in the lemon sauce until blended and pour over the chicken. Garnish with lemon slices.

Beef & Chilli Black Bean Sauce

You don't need to use expensive cuts of beef steak for this recipe: the meat will be tender as it is cut into thin slices and marinated.

SERVES 4

250–300 g/ 8–10 oz beef steak (such as rump)
1 small onion
1 small green (bell) pepper, cored and deseeded
about 300 ml/½ pint/ 1¼ cups vegetable oil
1 spring onion (scallion), cut into short sections
a few small slices of ginger root
1–2 small green or red chillies, deseeded and sliced
2 tbsp crushed black bean sauce

Marinade:
½ tsp bicarbonate of soda (baking soda) or baking powder
½ tsp sugar • 1 tbsp light soy sauce
2 tsp rice wine or dry sherry
2 tsp Cornflour (Cornstarch) Paste (see page 18)
2 tsp sesame oil

1 Cut the beef into thin strips. Mix the marinade ingredients in a shallow dish, add the beef strips, turn to coat and leave to marinate for at least 2–3 hours – the longer the better.

2 Cut the onion and green (bell) pepper into small equal-sized squares.

3 Heat the oil in a preheated wok. Add the beef strips and stir-fry for 1 minute, or until the colour changes. Remove with a slotted spoon and drain on paper towels. Keep warm.

4 Pour off the excess oil, leaving about 1 tablespoon in the wok.

Add the spring onion (scallion), ginger, chillies, onion and green (bell) pepper and stir-fry for about 1 minute. Add the black bean sauce, stir until smooth then return the beef strips to the wok. Blend well and stir-fry for 1 minute. Serve hot with boiled rice.

Oyster Sauce Beef

**As in Stir-Fried Pork with Vegetables
(page 44), the vegetables can be varied
as you wish.**

SERVES 4

*300 g/10 oz beef steak
1 tsp sugar • 1 tbsp light soy sauce
1 tsp rice wine or dry sherry
1 tsp Cornflour (Cornstarch) Paste (see page 18)
½ small carrot
60 g/2 oz mangetout (snow peas)
60 g/2 oz canned bamboo shoots
60 g/2 oz canned straw mushrooms
about 300 ml/½ pint/1¼ cups vegetable oil
1 spring onion (scallion), cut into short sections
2–3 small slices of ginger root • ½ tsp salt
2 tbsp oyster sauce
2–3 tbsp Chinese Stock (see page 20) or water*

1 Cut the beef into small, thin slices. Place in a shallow dish with the sugar, soy sauce, wine and cornflour (cornstarch) paste, turn to coat and leave to marinate for 25–30 minutes.

2 Slice the carrots, mangetout (snow peas), bamboo shoots and straw mushrooms so that as far as possible the vegetable pieces are of uniform size and thickness.

3 Heat the oil in a preheated wok and add the beef slices. Stir-fry for 1 minute, then remove with a slotted spoon and keep warm.

4 Pour off the excess oil, leaving about 1 tablespoon in the wok. Add the sliced vegetables with the spring onion (scallion) and ginger, and stir-fry for about 2 minutes. Add the salt, beef, oyster sauce and stock or water. Blend well until heated through, and serve.

Stir-Fried Pork with Vegetables

**This is a basic 'meat and veg' recipe –
using pork, chicken, beef or lamb, and
vegetables according to seasonal availability.**

SERVES 4

*250 g/ 8 oz pork fillet • 1 tsp sugar
1 tbsp light soy sauce • 1 tsp rice wine or dry sherry
1 tsp Cornflour (Cornstarch) Paste (see page 18)
1 small carrot
1 small green (bell) pepper, cored and deseeded
about 175 g/ 6 oz Chinese leaves • 4 tbsp vegetable oil
1 spring onion (scallion), cut into short sections
a few small slices of peeled ginger root • 1 tsp salt
2–3 tbsp Chinese Stock (see page 20) or water
a few drops of sesame oil*

1 Slice the pork fillet into small pieces and place in a shallow dish. Add half the sugar, half the soy sauce, the wine and cornflour (cornstarch) paste, turn to coat and leave in the refrigerator to marinate for 10–15 minutes.

2 Cut the carrot, green (bell) pepper and Chinese leaves into slices the same size as the pork pieces.

3 Heat the oil in a preheated wok and stir-fry the pork for about 1 minute to seal in the flavour. Remove with a slotted spoon and keep warm.

4 Add the carrot, (bell) pepper, Chinese leaves, spring onion (scallion) and ginger to the wok and stir-fry for 2 minutes. Add the salt and remaining sugar, followed by the pork and remaining soy sauce, and the stock or water. Blend and stir-fry for 1–2 minutes until hot. Sprinkle with the sesame oil and serve.

Egg Fried Rice

The rice used for frying should not be too soft. Ideally, the rice should have been slightly under-cooked and left to cool before frying.

SERVES 4

3 eggs
1 tsp salt
2 spring onions (scallions), finely chopped
2–3 tbsp vegetable oil
500 g/1 lb/3 cups cooked rice,
well drained and cooled (see note in step 3)
125 g/4 oz cooked peas

1 Lightly beat the eggs with a pinch of salt and 1 tablespoon of the spring onions (scallions).

2 Heat the oil in a preheated wok, add the eggs and stir until lightly scrambled. (The eggs should only be cooked until they start to set, so they are still moist.)

3 Add the rice and stir to make sure that each grain of rice is separated. Note: the cooked rice should be cool, preferably cold, so that much of the moisture has evaporated. This ensures that the oil will coat the grains of rice and prevent them sticking. Store the cooked rice in the refrigerator until ready to cook. Make sure the oil is really hot before adding the rice, to avoid the rice being saturated with oil, which will make it heavy and greasy.

4 Add the remaining salt, spring onions (scallions) and peas to the wok. Blend well and serve hot or cold.

Egg Fu-Yung with Rice

This dish is a great way of using up leftover cooked rice. It can be served as a meal by itself or as an accompaniment.

SERVES 2–4

175 g/ 6 oz/ ¾ cup long-grain rice
2 Chinese dried mushrooms (if unavailable, use thinly sliced open-cup mushrooms)
3 eggs, beaten • 3 tbsp vegetable oil
4 spring onions (scallions), sliced
½ green (bell) pepper, chopped
60 g/ 2 oz/ ⅓ cup canned bamboo shoots
60 g/ 2 oz/ ⅓ cup canned water chestnuts, sliced
125 g/ 4 oz/ 2 cups bean-sprouts
2 tbsp light soy sauce • 2 tbsp dry sherry
2 tsp sesame oil • salt and pepper

1 Cook the rice in lightly salted boiling water according to the instructions on the packet.

2 Place the dried mushrooms in a small bowl, cover with warm water and leave to soak for 20–25 minutes.

3 Mix the beaten eggs with a pinch of salt. Heat 1 tablespoon of the oil in a wok or large frying pan (skillet). Add the eggs and stir until just set. Remove and set aside.

4 Drain the mushrooms and squeeze out the excess water. Remove the tough centres and discard. Slice the mushrooms thinly.

5 Heat the remaining oil in a clean wok or frying pan (skillet). Add the mushrooms, spring onions (scallions) and green (bell) pepper, and stir-fry for 2 minutes. Add the bamboo shoots, water chestnuts and bean-sprouts. Stir-fry for 1 minute.

6 Drain the rice thoroughly and add to the pan with

the soy sauce, dry sherry and
sesame oil. Mix well, heating
the rice thoroughly. Season to
taste with salt and pepper.
Stir in the reserved eggs and
serve hot.

Fragrant Steamed Rice in Lotus Leaves

The fragrance of the lotus leaves penetrates the rice, giving it a unique taste.

SERVES 4

2 lotus leaves (if unavailable, use large cabbage or spinach leaves)
4 Chinese dried mushrooms (if unavailable, use thinly sliced open-cup mushrooms)
175 g/ 6 oz/ ³⁄₄ cup long-grain rice • 1 cinnamon stick
6 cardamom pods • 4 cloves
1 tsp salt • 2 eggs • 1 tbsp vegetable oil
2 spring onions (scallions), chopped • 1 tbsp soy sauce
2 tbsp sherry • 1 tsp sugar • 1 tsp sesame oil

1 Unfold the lotus leaves carefully and cut along the fold to divide each leaf in half. Lay on a large baking sheet (cookie sheet) and pour over enough hot water to cover. Leave to soak for about 30 minutes or until the leaves have softened.

2 Place the dried mushrooms in a small bowl and cover with warm water. Leave to soak for 20–25 minutes.

3 Cook the rice in a saucepan of boiling water with the cinnamon stick, cardamom pods, cloves and salt for about 10 minutes – the rice should be partially cooked. Drain well and remove the cinnamon stick.

4 Beat the eggs lightly. Heat the oil in a wok or frying pan (skillet) and cook the eggs quickly, stirring until set; then remove and set aside.

5 Drain the mushrooms, squeezing out the excess water. Remove the tough centres and discard, and chop the mushrooms. Place the drained rice in a bowl. Stir in the mushrooms, cooked egg,

spring onions (scallions), soy
sauce, sherry, sugar and
sesame oil. Season with salt.

6 Drain the lotus leaves and
divide the rice mixture
into 4 portions. Place a
portion in the centre of each

lotus leaf and fold up to form
a parcel (package). Place in a
steamer, cover and steam
over simmering water for
20 minutes. To serve, cut
the tops of the lotus leaves
open to expose the fragrant
rice inside.

Ma-Po Tofu (Bean Curd)

**Ma-Po, the wife of a Szechuan chef,
created this dish in the 19th century.
Replace the beef with dried mushrooms to
make a vegetarian meal.**

SERVES 4

3 cakes tofu (bean curd)
3 tbsp vegetable oil
125 g/ 4 oz coarsely minced (ground) beef
½ tsp finely chopped garlic
1 leek, cut into short sections
½ tsp salt
1 tbsp black bean sauce
1 tbsp light soy sauce
1 tsp chilli bean sauce
3–4 tbsp Chinese Stock (see page 20) or water
2 tsp Cornflour (Cornstarch) Paste (see page 18)
a few drops of sesame oil
black pepper
finely chopped spring onions (scallions), to garnish

1 Cut the tofu (bean curd) into 1 cm/½ inch cubes, handling it carefully. Bring some water to the boil in a pan or a wok, add the tofu (bean curd) and blanch for 2–3 minutes to harden. Remove and drain well.

2 Heat the oil in a preheated wok. Add the minced (ground) beef and garlic, and stir-fry for 1 minute, or until the beef changes colour. Add the leek, salt and sauces, and blend well. Add the stock or water and the tofu (bean curd). Bring to the boil and braise for 2–3 minutes.

3 Add the cornflour (cornstarch) paste, and stir until the sauce has thickened. Sprinkle with sesame oil and black pepper, and garnish with spring onions (scallions).

Singapore-Style Rice Noodles

Rice noodles, or vermicelli, are also known as rice sticks. Egg noodles can be used for this dish, but it will not taste quite the same.

SERVES 4

200 g/7 oz rice vermicelli
125 g/4 oz cooked chicken or pork
60 g/2 oz peeled prawns (shrimp), defrosted if frozen
4 tbsp vegetable oil
1 onion, shredded thinly
125 g/4 oz/2 cups fresh bean-sprouts
1 tsp salt
1 tbsp mild curry powder
2 tbsp light soy sauce
2 spring onions (scallions), shredded thinly
1–2 small fresh green or red chilli peppers, deseeded and shredded thinly

1 Soak the rice vermicelli in boiling water for 8–10 minutes, then rinse in cold water and drain well.

2 Thinly slice the cooked meat. Dry the prawns (shrimp) on paper towels.

3 Heat the oil in a preheated wok. Add the onion and stir-fry until opaque. Add the bean-sprouts and stir-fry for 1 minute.

4 Add the noodles with the meat and prawns (shrimp), and continue stir-frying for 1 minute.

5 Blend in the salt, curry powder and soy sauce, followed by the spring onions (scallions) and chilli peppers. Stir-fry for 1 minute, then serve immediately.

Gingered Broccoli with Orange

Thinly sliced broccoli florets are lightly stir-fried and served in a ginger and orange sauce.

SERVES 4

750 g/ 1½ lb broccoli
2 thin slices of ginger root
2 garlic cloves
1 orange
2 tsp cornflour (cornstarch)
1 tbsp light soy sauce
½ tsp sugar
2 tbsp vegetable oil

1 Divide the broccoli into small florets. Peel the stems, using a vegetable peeler, and then cut the stems into thin slices. Cut the ginger root into matchsticks and slice the garlic.

2 Peel 2 strips of zest from the orange and cut into strips. Place the strips in a bowl, cover with water and set aside. Squeeze the juice from the orange and mix with the cornflour (cornstarch), soy sauce. sugar and 4 tablespoons of water.

3 Heat the oil in a wok or frying pan (skillet). Add the sliced broccoli stems and stir-fry for 2 minutes. Add the ginger root, garlic and broccoli florets, and stir-fry for 3 minutes.

4 Stir in the orange sauce mixture and cook, stirring constantly, until the sauce has thickened and coated the broccoli. Drain the reserved orange zest and stir into the wok or pan before serving.

Braised Chinese Leaves

White cabbage can be used instead of Chinese leaves for this dish. Try to use the correct type of peppercorns in preparing the recipe. Szechuan red peppercorns have a pungent, aromatic odour which distinguishes them from the hotter black peppercorns. Roast them briefly in the oven or sauté them in a dry frying pan (skillet), then grind them in a spice grinder or pestle and mortar and store in a jar until needed.

SERVES 4

500 g/ 1 lb Chinese leaves or firm white cabbage
3 tbsp vegetable oil
½ tsp Szechuan peppercorns
5–6 small dried red chillies, deseeded and chopped
½ tsp salt
1 tbsp sugar
1 tbsp light soy sauce
1 tbsp rice vinegar
a few drops of sesame oil (optional)

1 Shred the Chinese leaves or cabbage crossways into thin pieces. (If using firm-packed white cabbage, cut out and discard the thick core before shredding the leaves.)

2 Heat the oil in a preheated wok, add the Szechuan peppercorns and the dried chillies and stir-fry for a few seconds.

3 Add the Chinese leaves or white cabbage to the peppercorns and chillies, stir-fry for about 1 minute, then add the salt and continue stir-frying for 1 minute.

4 Add the sugar, soy sauce and vinegar, blend well and stir-fry for 1 minute. Sprinkle with the sesame oil, if using. Serve hot or cold.

Index